FALL RIVER PRESS

New York

An Imprint of Sterling Publishing
387 Park Avenue South
New York, NY 10016

This 2006 edition published by Fall River Press by arrangement with
Lagoon Trading Company Limited.

ISBN 978-0-7607-7962-0

Distributed in Canada by Sterling Publishing
c/o Canadian Manda Group, 165 Dufferin Street
Toronto, Ontario, Canada M6K 3H6
Distributed in the United Kingdom by GMC Distribution Services
Castle Place, 166 High Street, Lewes, East Sussex, England BN7 1XU
Distributed in Australia by Capricorn Link (Australia) Pty. Ltd.
P.O. Box 704, Windsor, NSW 2756, Australia

For information about custom editions, special sales, and premium and corporate
purchases, please contact Sterling Special Sales at 800-805-5489 or
specialsales@sterlingpublishing.com.

Manufactured in China

6 8 10 9 7

www.sterlingpublishing.com

TRIVIA FOR THE TOILET

Gavin Webster

FALL RIVER PRESS

New York

Trivia is the Roman goddess of sorcery, hounds, and crossroads.

A cough releases an explosive charge of air that moves at speeds of up to 60 m.p.h.

Mexico City, the oldest capital city in the Americas, is sinking at a rate of six to eight inches a year because it's built on top of an underground reservoir. Wells are drawing out more and more water for the city's growing population of more than 15 million people.

Britain's present royal family was originally named Saxe-Coburg-Gotha. The name was changed in 1917, during World War I, because of its German connotations. The name Windsor was suggested by one of the staff. At the same time their cousins, the Battenberg family, changed their name to Mountbatten.

From the 1500s to the 1700s, tobacco was prescribed by doctors to treat a variety of ailments including headaches, toothaches, arthritis, and bad breath.

The shortest war on record was fought between Zanzibar and the UK in 1896. Zanzibar surrendered after 38 minutes.

When Bugs Bunny first appeared in 1935, he was called Happy Rabbit.

People who laugh a lot are much healthier than those who don't. Dr. Lee Berk at the Loma Linda School of Public Health in California found that laughing lowers levels of stress hormones, and strengthens the immune system. Six-year-olds laugh an average of 300 times a day. Adults laugh only 15 to 100 times a day.

"Long in the tooth," meaning "old," was originally used to describe horses. As horses age, their gums recede, giving the impression that their teeth are growing. The longer the teeth look, the older the horse. You can also tell the sex of a horse by its teeth. Most males have 40, females have 36.

Chocolate contains phenylethylamine (PEA), a natural substance that is reputed to stimulate the same reaction in the body as falling in love. Consumers spend more than $7 billion a year on chocolate. Annual per capita consumption of chocolate in the U.S. is 12 pounds per person. Chocolate not only does not promote tooth decay; it may prevent it. According to the American Dental Association, milk chocolate contains ingredients, such as calcium and phosphate, that might modify acid production in the mouth that leads to cavities. Some oils in chocolate might also prevent tooth decay. Chocolate does contain sugar, of course, but these are simple sugars that are less harmful than the complex sugars contained in other foods.

Humans shed about 600,000 particles of skin every hour—about 1.5 pounds a year. By 70 years of age, an average person will have lost 105 pounds of skin.

Damascus, Syria, was flourishing a couple of thousand years before Rome was founded in 753 B.C., making it the oldest continuously inhabited city in existence.

A poll of 3,000 Americans found that for 41 percent, the thing they're most afraid of is speaking before a group of people. Thirty-two percent stated they were most afraid of heights.

Until 1965, driving was done on the left-hand side on roads in Sweden. The conversion to the right-hand side was done on a weekday at 5 P.M. All traffic stopped as people switched sides. The time and day were chosen to prevent accidents where drivers would have gotten up in the morning and been too sleepy to realize this was the day of the changeover.

The oldest living thing in existence is not a giant redwood, but a bristlecone pine in the White Mountains of California, estimated to be 4,600 years old.

The yo-yo was introduced in 1929 by Donald F. Duncan. The toy was based on a weapon used by 16th-century Filipino hunters.

The English word "soup" comes from the Middle Ages word "sop" which means a slice of bread over which roast drippings were poured. The first archeological evidence of soup being consumed dates back to 6000 B.C., with the main ingredient being hippopotamus bones.

A "jiffy" is an actual unit of time for 1/100 of a second.

Armored knights raised their visors to identify themselves when they rode past their king. This custom has become the modern military salute.

Absolutely pure gold is so soft that it can be molded with the hands. A lump of pure gold the size of a matchbox can be flattened into a sheet the size of a tennis court. An ounce of gold can be stretched into a wire 50 miles long.

Barbers at one time combined shaving and haircutting with bloodletting and pulling teeth. The white stripes on a field of red that spiral down a barber pole represent the bandages used in the bloodletting.

There are 45 miles of nerves in the skin of a human being.

Money isn't made out of paper—it's made out of linen.

Natural gas has no odor. The smell is added artificially so that leaks can be detected.

While known as a painter, sculptor, architect, and engineer, Leonardo da Vinci was the first to record that the number of rings in the cross-section of a tree trunk reveals its age. He also discovered that the width between the rings indicates the annual moisture. He could write with one hand and draw with the other at the same time. Despite his great scientific and artistic achievement, he was proudest of his ability to bend iron with his bare hands.

The National Oceanic and Atmospheric Administration announced in 1978 that it would alternate men's and women's names in the naming of hurricanes. It was seen as an attempt at fair play. Hurricanes had been named for women for years, until the NOAA succumbed to pressure from women's groups, who were demanding that Atlantic storms be given unisex names.

In the Netherlands, in 1634, a collector paid 1,000 pounds of cheese, four oxen, eight pigs, 12 sheep, a bed, and a suit of clothes for a single bulb of the Viceroy tulip.

In 1945, a computer at Harvard malfunctioned and Grace Hopper, who was working on the computer, investigated, found a moth in one of the circuits, and removed it. Ever since, when something goes wrong with a computer, it is said to have a bug in it.

The first city to reach a population of one million people was Rome, in 133 B.C. London reached the mark in 1810, and New York made it in 1875. Today, there are over 300 cities in the world that boast a population in excess of one million.

Mayonnaise is said to be the invention of the French chef of the Duke de Richelieu in 1756. While the Duke was defeating the British at Port Mahon, his chef was creating a victory feast that included a sauce made of cream and eggs. When the chef realized that there was no cream in the kitchen, he improvised, substituting olive oil for the cream. A new culinary masterpiece was born, and the chef named it "Mahonnaise" in honor of the Duke's victory.

The average human body contains enough iron to make a six-inch nail, sulfur to kill all the fleas on an average dog, carbon to make 900 pencils, potassium to fire a toy cannon, fat to make seven bars of soap, phosphorus to make 2,200 match heads, and water to fill a ten-gallon tank.

The kiss that is given by the bride to the groom at the end of the wedding ceremony originates from the earliest times when the couple would actually make love for the first time under the eyes of half the village!

The world's tallest mountains, the Himalayas, are also the fastest growing. Their growth—about half-an-inch a year—is caused by the pressure exerted by two of the Earth's continental plates (the Eurasian plate and the Indo-Australian plate) pushing against one another.

The term "honeymoon" is derived from the Babylonians who declared mead, a honey-flavored wine, the official wedding drink, stipulating that the bride's parents be required to keep the groom supplied with the drink for the month following the wedding.

Eighty-four percent of a raw apple is water. A cucumber is 96 percent water.

The sandwich is named for the Fourth Earl of Sandwich (1718–92), for whom sandwiches were made so that he could stay at the gambling table without interruptions for meals.

False eyelashes were invented by the American film director D. W. Griffith while he was making his 1916 epic, *Intolerance*. Griffith wanted actress Seena Owen to have lashes that brushed her cheeks, to make her eyes shine larger than life. A wigmaker wove human hair through fine gauze, which was then gummed to Owen's eyelids. *Intolerance* was critically acclaimed but flopped financially, leaving Griffith with huge debts that he might have been able to settle easily—had he only thought to patent the eyelashes.

The most abundant metal in the Earth's crust is aluminum. The Chinese were using aluminum to make things as early as 300 A.D., although Western civilization didn't rediscover aluminum until 1827. Napoleon III provided his most honored guests with knives and forks made of pure aluminum. At the time the newly discovered metal was so rare, it was considered more valuable than gold.

The first performance of Handel's *Messiah* was on April 13, 1742, at the New Music rooms in Fishamble Street, Dublin. Because of the demand for space, the men were asked not to wear their swords and the ladies not to wear hooped skirts.

More than 99.9 percent of all the animal species that have ever lived on Earth were extinct before the coming of man.

The Great Lakes are Lake Michigan, Lake Huron, Lake Superior, Lake Erie, and Lake Ontario. They form the most important inland waterway in North America. All the lakes, except Lake Michigan, which lies entirely in the United States, are shared by the United States and Canada and form part of the border between these countries. They contain six quadrillion gallons of fresh water, one fifth of the world's fresh surface water. The Great Lakes have a total area of 94,230 square miles— larger than the states of New York, New Jersey, Connecticut, Rhode Island, Massachusetts, and Vermont combined.

The first safety feature for an automobile was invented in 1908 by John O'Leary. He patented a large net, to be installed on the front bumper, to scoop pedestrians out of the way before they could be run over.

Rudolph, the Red-Nosed Reindeer, was created in 1939, in Chicago, for the Montgomery Ward department stores for a Christmas promotion. The lyrics were written as a poem by Robert May, but weren't set to music until 1947. Gene Autry recorded the hit song in 1949.

The first toothbrush with bristles was developed in China in 1498. Bristles were taken from hogs at first, later from horses. The nylon bristles were developed in 1938 by DuPont.

The ancient Egyptians slept on pillows made of stone.

The world's smallest independent state is Vatican City, with a population of about 1,000—and a zero birthrate. The Vatican's Swiss Guard still wears a uniform designed by Michelangelo in the early 16th century.

The word "news" came from the first letters of the words North, East, West, and South. This was because information was being gathered from all different directions.

About one-tenth of the Earth's surface is permanently covered with ice.

Chocolate syrup was used for blood in the famous 45-second shower scene in Alfred Hitchcock's movie, *Psycho*, which actually took seven days to shoot.

The color of a chili is no indication of its spiciness, but size usually is—the smaller the pepper, the hotter it is. Capsaicin, which makes hot peppers "hot" to the human mouth, is best neutralized by casein, the main protein found in milk.

Each king in a deck of playing cards represents a great king from history: Spades—King David, Clubs—Alexander the Great, Hearts—Charlemagne, Diamonds—Julius Caesar.

Although construction of the Notre Dame Cathedral in Strasbourg started in 1015, it was not until 1439 that the spire was completed.

In Great Britain and the American colonies the year 1752 had only 354 days. In that year, the type of calendar was changed, and 11 days were lost.

Americans eat more bananas than any other fruit, a total of 11 billion a year. Bananas are actually herbs and die after fruiting, like all herbs do.

As many as nine out of ten people are right-handed, and the word for that side, "right," is derived from a variety of sources, all of which suggest strength. "Left," on the other hand, comes from the Old English, *lyft*, for useless, weak. Left-handed people are statistically more likely to be geniuses, and to be insane. Left-handedness is more common among writers and some kinds of artists. Gerald Ford, George Bush, John F. Kennedy, Jr., Paul McCartney, Ringo Starr, and Bill Clinton are well-known left-handers.

A newborn kangaroo is about one inch in length. An adult kangaroo can leap over 30 feet in one bound.

"Ough" can be pronounced in eight different ways. The following sentence contains them all: "A tough, dough-faced ploughman strode through the streets of Scarborough, coughing and hiccoughing thoughtfully."

A typical lightning bolt is two to four inches wide and two miles long.

Clans of long ago that wanted to get rid of their unwanted people without killing them used to burn their houses down — hence the expression "to get fired."

The largest single flower is the rafflesia, or "corpse flower." It is generally three feet in diameter, with the record being 42 inches.

The world's costliest coffee, at $130 a pound, is called *kopi luwak*. It is found in the droppings of a type of marsupial that eats only the very best coffee beans. Plantation workers track them and scoop up their precious poop.

In the 19th century, craftsmen who made hats were known to be excitable and irrational, as well as to tremble with palsy and mix up their words. Such behavior gave rise to the familiar expression "mad as a hatter." The disorder, called hatter's shakes, was caused by chronic mercury poisoning from the solution used to treat the felt. Attacking the central nervous system, the toxin led to behavioral symptoms.

In 1984, a Canadian farmer began renting advertising space on his cows.

Canada is a Native American word meaning "Big Village."

Persians first began using colored eggs to celebrate spring in 3,000 B.C. Thirteenth-century Macedonians were the first Christians on record to use colored eggs in Easter celebrations. Crusaders returning from the Middle East spread the custom of coloring eggs, and Europeans began to use them to celebrate Easter and other warm-weather holidays.

The longest-reigning monarch in history was Pepi II, who ruled Egypt for 90 years: 2566 to 2476 B.C. The second longest was France's Louis XIV, who ruled for 72 years: 1643 to 1715.

A rat can last longer without water than a camel can.

Ancient Egyptians believed that Bast was the mother of all cats on Earth. They also believed that cats were sacred animals. The penalty for killing a cat was death. In ancient Egypt, entire families would shave their eyebrows as a sign of mourning when the family cat died.

Dueling is legal in Paraguay as long as both parties are registered blood donors.

The plant life in the oceans makes up about 85 percent of all the greenery on the Earth.

The song "Happy Birthday to You" was originally written by sisters Mildred and Patty Hill as "Good Morning to You." The words were changed and it was published in 1935.

Saffron, made from the dried stamens of cultivated crocus flowers, is the most expensive cooking spice.

The average person falls asleep in seven minutes and is about a quarter-of-an-inch taller at night.

Oak trees do not produce acorns until they are at least fifty years old.

The White House, in Washington, D.C., was initially gray, the color of its original stone. After the War of 1812, during which it had been burned by Canadian troops, the outside walls were painted white to hide the smoke stains.

Adult cats with no health problems are in deep sleep 15 percent of their lives. They are in light sleep 50 percent of the time.

The phrase "sleep tight" originated when mattresses were set upon ropes woven through the bed frame. To remedy sagging ropes, one would use a bed key to tighten the rope.

The Hollywood sign was first erected in 1923. Conceived as a real estate ad, it originally read "Hollywoodland." The sign stands 50-feet tall, stretches 450-feet across, and weighs 450,000 pounds.

In 4000 B.C., Egyptian men and women wore glitter eye-shadow made from the crushed shells of beetles.

In 1920, 57 percent of Hollywood movies billed the female star above the leading man. In 1990, only 18 percent gave the leading lady top billing.

Diamonds are crystals formed virtually entirely of carbon. Because of its hardness, the diamond is the most enduring of all gemstones. They are among the most costly jewels in the world, partly because they are rare. Only four important diamond fields have been found—in Africa, South America, India, and the former Soviet Union. The Cullinan Diamond was the largest gem-quality diamond ever discovered. Found in 1905, the original 3,100 carats were cut to make jewels for the British Crown Jewels and the British royal family's collection.

Yellowstone is the world's first national park. It was dedicated in 1872.

The fungi called truffles can cost $800 to $1,500 per pound. They are sniffed out by female pigs, which detect a compound that is also found in the saliva of male pigs. The same chemical is found in the sweat of human males.

An ostrich's eye is bigger than its brain.

Beards are the fastest growing hairs on the human body. If the average man never trimmed his beard, it would grow nearly 30-feet long in his lifetime.

Mao Zedong, like many Chinese people of his time, refused to brush his teeth. Instead, he rinsed his mouth with tea and chewed the leaves. Why brush? "Does a tiger brush his teeth?" asked Mao. Chairman Mao also loved to chain-smoke English cigarettes. When his doctor asked him to cut down, he explained, "Smoking is also a form of deep-breathing exercise, don't you think?"

Cats have better memories than dogs. Tests conducted by the University of Michigan concluded that while a dog's memory lasts no more than five minutes, a cat's can last as long as 16 hours—exceeding even that of monkeys and orangutans.

The term "dog days" dates back to Roman times, when it was believed that Sirius, the Dog Star, added its heat to that of the sun from July 3 to August 11, creating exceptionally high temperatures. The Romans called the period *dies caniculares*, or "days of the dog."

No species of wild plant produces a flower or blossom that is absolutely black, and so far none has been developed artificially.

All pet hamsters are descended from a single female wild golden hamster found with a litter of 12 young in Syria in 1930.

The largest item on any menu in the world is probably the roast camel, sometimes served at Bedouin wedding feasts. The camel is stuffed with a sheep's carcass, which is stuffed with chickens, which are stuffed with fish, which are stuffed with eggs.

The Romans had three words for kissing: *basium* was the kiss exchanged by acquaintances, *osculum*, the kiss between close friends, and *suavium*, the kiss between lovers.

On average, a woman utters around 7,000 words in a day while a man uses just over 2,000.

An adult lion's roar can be heard up to five miles away, and warns off intruders or reunites scattered members of the pride.

A fingernail or toenail takes about six months to grow from base to tip.

The first time the "f-word" was spoken in a film was by Marianne Faithfull in 1968 in *I'll Never Forget Whatshisname*. In Brian De Palma's 1984 film, *Scarface*, the word is spoken 206 times—an average of once every 29 seconds.

Carnivorous animals will not eat another animal that has been hit by a lightning bolt.

In 1492, Pope Innocent VIII drank the blood of three young donors thinking it would prevent aging and died shortly after.

In an authentic Chinese meal, the last course is soup because it allows the roast duck entrée to "swim" toward digestion.

If Monaco's ruling house of Grimaldi should ever be without an heir (male or female), the country will cease to be a sovereign state.

The Black Death reduced the population of Europe by one-third in the period from 1347 to 1351. Fourteenth-century physicians didn't know what caused the plague, but they knew it was contagious. As a result they wore an early kind of bioprotective suit which included a large beaked headpiece. The beak of the headpiece, which made them look like large birds, was filled with vinegar, sweet oils, and other strong smelling compounds to counteract the stench of the dead and dying plague victims.

The word gargoyle comes down from the Old French, *gargouille*, meaning throat or gullet. This is also the origin of the word gargle. The word describes the sound produced as water passes the throat and mixes with air. In early architecture, gargoyles were decorative creatures on the drains of cathedrals.

In most American states, a wedding ring is exempt by law from inclusion among the assets in a bankruptcy estate. This means that a wedding ring cannot be seized by creditors, no matter how much the bankrupt person owes.

The average human produces 25,000 quarts of spit in a lifetime, enough to fill two swimming pools.

Elvis Presley wore a cross, a Star of David, and the Hebrew letter *chi*. He explained his jewelry habit with, "I don't want to miss out on heaven due to a technicality."

An American Animal Hospital Association poll showed that 33 percent of dog owners admit that they talk to their dogs on the phone or leave messages on an answering machine while away.

97.2 percent of all the Earth's water is saltwater. There is enough salt in the world's oceans to cover all the continents with a layer 492-feet thick.

The phrase "rule of thumb" is derived from an old English law which stated that you couldn't beat your wife with anything wider than your thumb.

Willow bark, which provides the salicylic acid from which aspirin was originally synthesized, has been used as a pain remedy ever since the Greeks discovered its therapeutic power nearly 2,500 years ago.

Ten percent of the salt mined in the world each year is used to de-ice the roads in America.

Large doses of coffee can be lethal. Ten grams, or 100 cups, over four hours, can kill the average human being.

A bride stands to the groom's left at a wedding so that his sword hand would be free. Apparently, Anglo-Saxon brides were often kidnapped before a wedding and brawls were common. That's also why the best man stands with the groom; the tribe's best warrior was there to help the groom defend the bride.

The largest U.S. city in area is Juneau, Alaska, which covers 3,108 square miles. Los Angeles covers only 458.2 square miles.

The vocabulary of the average person consists of 5,000 to 6,000 words.

Perfume contains ethyl alcohol and 25 percent fragrant oils. Cologne is cheaper to produce and to purchase because the oil content in cologne is only three percent. Cologne was named for the German city in which it was first produced. The original formula combined alcohol, lemon spirits, orange bitters, and mint oil.

The answer to the question, "Who wrote the Bible?" is, of course, Shakespeare. The King James Version was published in 1611. Shakespeare was 46 years old then (he turned 47 later in the year). Look up Psalm 46. Count 46 words from the beginning of the Psalm. You will find the word "Shake." Count 46 words from the end of the Psalm. You will find the word "Spear." An obvious coded message.

A cat will clean itself with paw and tongue after a dangerous experience or when it has fought with another cat. This is believed to be an attempt by the animal to soothe its nerves by doing something natural and instinctive.

In the Middle Ages, young men and women drew names from a bowl to see who their valentines would be. They would wear these names on their sleeves for one week. To wear your heart on your sleeve now means that it is easy for other people to know how you are feeling.

Babies are born with about 300 bones, but by adulthood we have only 206 bones in our bodies.

With 980-plus species, bats make up more than 23 percent of all known mammals by species.

The world's first speed limit was in the UK in 1903.
It was 20 m.p.h.

The rose family of plants, in addition to flowers, gives us apples, pears, plums, cherries, almonds, peaches, and apricots.

Mockingbirds can imitate any sound from a squeaking door to a cat meowing.

When Swiss cheese ferments, a bacterial action generates gas. As the gas is liberated, it bubbles through the cheese leaving holes. Cheese-makers call them "eyes."

Dogs do not sweat by salivating. They sweat through the pads of their feet.

In 1991 Procter & Gamble won a $75,000 lawsuit against James and Linda Newton who were found responsible for spreading rumors that the company supported the Church of Satan. The two were distributors of Amway Products, a competitor of Procter & Gamble.

A father sea catfish keeps the eggs of his young in his mouth until they are ready to hatch. He will not eat until his young are born, which may take several weeks.

A mole can dig a tunnel 300-feet long in one night.

If you commute to work every day, taking an hour to get to work and an hour to return home, between the ages of 22 and 65 you will have spent two-and-a-half years in transit.

Mosquitoes prefer children to adults, and blondes to brunettes. Eating bananas increases your chances of being bitten by a mosquito.

By the age of sixty, most people have lost half of their taste buds.

The world's deadliest mushroom is the *Amanita phalloides*, the death cap. The five different poisons contained by the mushroom cause diarrhea and vomiting within six to twelve hours of ingestion. This is followed by damage to the liver, kidneys, and central nervous system—and, in the majority of cases, coma and death.

In the U.S., a reward of $1,000 was offered for information leading to the capture and conviction of a man robbing taxi drivers. The man turned himself in and demanded the reward as a result. He received a 20-year sentence for aggravated robbery instead.

Humans shed and regrow outer skin cells about every 27 days—the equivalent of almost 1,000 new skins in a lifetime.

Sharks are apparently the only animals that never fall ill. As far as is known, they are immune to every known disease, including cancer.

Cats step with both left legs, then both right legs, when they walk or run. The only other animals to do this are the giraffe and the camel.

The correct response to the Irish greeting, "Top of the morning to you" is "And the rest of the day to yourself."

More people suffer heart attacks and more cars break down on Monday than on any other day of the week, while 50 percent of all bank robberies take place on Friday.

If it were removed from the body, the small intestine would stretch to a length of 22 feet.

Roy C. Sullivan of Virginia was struck by lightning seven times in his life. He suffered a burnt left shoulder, burnt legs, chest, and stomach, burnt hair (twice), and lost a toenail and both eyebrows.

Every known dog except the chow has a pink tongue—the chow's tongue is jet black.

The robbery phrase "hands up" originated in British Columbia. Bill Miner, an American known as the Gentleman Bandit, is said to have first used the phrase while robbing a Canadian Pacific Railways train in Mission Junction, British Columbia, in 1904.

Because Napoleon believed that armies marched on their stomachs, he offered a prize in 1795 for a practical way of preserving food. The prize was won by a French inventor, Nicholas Appert. What he devised was canning. It was the beginning of the canned food industry of today.

The Spanish Inquisition once condemned the entire Netherlands to death for heresy.

While sleeping, one man in eight snores, and one in ten grinds his teeth. The sound of a snore (up to 69 decibels) can be almost as loud as the noise of a pneumatic drill.

Before the enactment of the 1978 law that made it mandatory for dog owners in New York City to clean up after their pets, approximately 40 million pounds of dog excrement were deposited on the streets every year.

The short-term memory capacity for most people is between five and nine items or digits. This is one reason that phone numbers were kept to seven digits for so long.

During his or her lifetime, the average human will grow 590 miles of hair.

In Redondo Beach, California, a police officer arrested a driver after a short chase and charged him with drunk driving. Officer Joseph Fonteno's suspicions were aroused when he saw the white Mazda MX-7 rolling down Pacific Coast Highway with half of a traffic-light pole, including the lights, lying across its hood. The driver had hit the pole and simply kept on driving. According to Fonteno, when the driver was asked about the pole, he said, "It came with the car when I bought it."

A spider's web is made of two types of silk, one sticky and the other not. The spider begins the web with the non-sticky silk and forms the "spokes." After the frame is constructed and secure, the spider goes back with the sticky silk and completes the web design we are so familiar with, connecting spoke to spoke. It will also add rows connecting the spokes to allow access for web maintenance. Spend time watching a spider and you will see that it painstakingly avoids the sticky silk and walks on the spokes. Should the spider be startled and walk on the sticky silk it will stick to the spider the same as it would to anything else. Spiders recycle their webbing, so a spider that gets stuck in its own web may eat its way out.

Crossing one's fingers is a way of secretly making the Sign of the Cross. It was started by early Christians to ask for divine assistance without attracting the attention of pagans.

In the marriage ceremony of the ancient Incas of Peru, the couple was considered officially wed when they took off their sandals and handed them to each other.

The silkworm's silk comes out of its mouth as a thread of gooey liquid, so that nice silk blouse you spent a fortune on is really just worm spit.

A woman from Linthicum, Maryland, dressed only in her underwear, lost her balance while putting down linoleum in her home and fell smack into the glue that was spread on the floor, according to Battalion Chief John M. Scholz of the County Fire Department. She became stuck to the floor (mistake one) but somehow managed to free herself after a while and called the emergency number 911. When the ambulance crew arrived they found her sitting on her couch (mistake number two). She was now glued to her couch. She had crossed her legs (mistake number three). Her legs were now glued together. And they also found her cordless phone glued to her hand. Using solvent-dipped sterile gauze pads, they eventually freed her legs, hands, and extremities. She refused to be taken to the hospital.

The mummified hand of a notary public, chopped off for falsely certifying a document, has been on display in the city hall of Munster, Germany, as a warning to other notaries, for 400 years.

Undertakers report that human bodies do not deteriorate as quickly as they used to. The reason, they believe, is that the modern diet contains so many preservatives that these chemicals tend to prevent the body from decomposition too rapidly after death.

The longest place-name still in use is Taumatawhakatangihangakoauauotamateaturipukakapiki-maungahoronukupokaiwe-nuakit natahu, a New Zealand hill.

Peter Karpin, a German espionage agent in World War I, was seized by French Intelligence agents in 1914 as soon as he entered the country. Keeping his capture a secret, the French sent faked reports from Karpin to Germany and intercepted the agent's wages and expense money until Karpin escaped in 1917. With those funds the French purchased a car, which, in 1919, in the occupied Ruhr, accidentally ran down and killed a man, who proved to be Peter Karpin.

A slander case in Thailand was once settled by a witness who said nothing at all. According to the memoirs of Justice Gerald Sparrow, a 20th-century British barrister who served as a judge in Bangkok, the case involved two rival Chinese merchants, Pu Lin and Swee Ho. Pu Lin had stated sneeringly at a party that Swee Ho's new wife, Li Bua, was merely a decoration to show how rich her husband was. Swee Ho, he said, could no longer "please the ladies." Swee Ho sued for slander, claiming Li Bua was his wife in every sense—and he won his case, along with substantial damages, without a word of evidence being taken. Swee Ho's lawyer simply put the blushing bride in the witness box. She had decorative, gold-painted fingernails, to be sure, but she was also quite obviously pregnant.

The duration record for a face-slapping contest was set in Kiev, USSR, in 1931, when a draw was declared between Bezbordny and Goniusch after 30 hours.

The largest employer in the world is the Indian railway system, which employs over a million people.

In Milan, Italy, there is a law on the books that requires a smile on the face of all citizens at all times. Exemptions include time spent visiting patients in hospitals or attending funerals. Otherwise, citizens may be fined if they are seen in public without smiles on their faces.

In Boise, Idaho, a woman's getaway was ruined when she ran out of the pharmacy she had just robbed and jumped into what she thought was a taxi. It was a police car.

Jeanne Pierre François Blanchard built the first parachute and tested it using a dog. He put the dog in a basket equipped with his invention and then dropped it from a hot air balloon. It was a giant step forward for aviation history, but a giant step backwards in establishing the dog as man's best friend.

Fluoridated toothpaste came about as the result of a discovery made in Naples, Italy, in 1802, when local dentists noticed yellowish-brown spots on their patient's teeth—but no cavities. Subsequent examination revealed that high levels of fluoride in the water caused the spots and prevented tooth decay, and that less fluoride protected teeth without causing the spots. It took a while for the discovery to be implemented; the first U.S. fluoridated water tests didn't take place until 1915, and Crest, the first toothpaste with fluoride in it, didn't hit the shops until 1956.

The mother of all mothers? The largest number of children born to one woman is recorded at 69. From 1725 to 1765 a Russian peasant woman gave birth to 16 sets of twins, seven sets of triplets, and four sets of quadruplets.

A Chilean man who has been stopped from voting in three elections because officials keep insisting he is dead said he was tired of arguing and would never try to vote again. "I'm tired of complaining without any success. I think this is the last time I am going to bother," said Ernesto Alvear, 74. For the third time Alvear was told by officials in the city of Valparaiso that he could not vote because, officially, he had been dead for almost ten years. The mix-up was due to the death of another man with the same name, forcing Alvear to provide skeptical officials with documents proving he is alive.

Because he felt such an important tool should be public property, English chemist John Walker never patented his invention—matches.

Jackie Bibby holds the record for sitting in a bathtub with the most live rattlesnakes. He sat in a tub with 35 of them.

The biggest bell is the "Tsar Kolokol," cast in the Kremlin in 1733. It weighs 216 tons but, alas, is cracked and has never been rung. The bell was being stored in a Moscow shed which caught fire. To save it, caretakers decided to throw water on the bell. This did not succeed, as the water hit the superheated metal and a giant piece immediately cracked off, destroying the bell forever.

The reason one wears a wedding ring on the third finger is that (tradition says) there is supposed to be a vein which goes directly from that finger to the heart—the seat of love. Not everyone wears their wedding ring on the third finger of the left hand. In some traditions, such as the Jewish one, it is worn on the right hand.

Snoring is prohibited in Massachusetts unless all bedroom windows are closed and securely locked. It is also illegal to go to bed without first having a full bath.

When christening a ship, instead of using champagne, the Vikings would sacrifice a human being. The Vikings also thought the spirit of the murdered person would guide and guard the craft.

George Washington died the last hour of the last day of the last week of the last month of the last year of the 18th century.

If two flies were left to reproduce without predators or other limitations for one year, the resulting mass of flies would be the size of the Earth.

Human blood travels 60,000 miles per day on its journey through the arteries, arterioles, and capillaries, and back through the venules and veins.

In 1970, Russel T. Tansie, an Arizona lawyer, filed a $100,000 damage lawsuit against God. The suit was filed on behalf of Mr. Tansie's secretary, Betty Penrose, who accused God of negligence in His power over the weather when He allowed a lightning bolt to strike her home. Ms. Penrose won the case when the defendant failed to appear in court. Whether or not she collected has not been recorded.

The reason firehouses have circular stairways is from the days of yore when the engines were pulled by horses. The horses were stabled on the ground floor and worked out how to walk up straight staircases.

In Saudi Arabia, a woman reportedly may divorce her husband if he does not keep her supplied with coffee.

Women shoplift more often than men; the statistics are four to one.

King Alfonso of Spain (1886–1931) was so tone-deaf that he had one man in his employ known as the Anthem Man. This man's duty was to tell the king to stand up whenever the Spanish national anthem was played, because the monarch couldn't recognize it.

Seoul, the South Korean capital, just means "the capital" in the Korean language.

The term "devil's advocate" comes from the Roman Catholic Church. When deciding if someone should be sainted, a devil's advocate is always appointed to give an alternative view.

Dr. Samuel Langley was able to get many model airplanes to fly, but on December 8, 1903, Langley's "human-carrying flying machine" plunged into the Potomac River near Washington, D.C., in front of photographers who were assembled to witness the event. Reporters around the country made fun of the idea that people could fly, and nine days later Wilbur and Orville Wright proved them wrong.

The human kidney consists of over one million little tubes with a total length of about 40 miles in both kidneys. The kidneys filter about 500 gallons of blood each day.

In Greek culture, brides carry a lump of sugar in their wedding glove. It's supposed to bring sweetness to their married life.

During the time that the atomic bomb was being hatched by the United States at Alamogordo, New Mexico, applicants for routine jobs like cleaners were disqualified if they could read—illiteracy was a job requirement. The reason: the authorities did not want their rubbish or other papers read.

Snails produce a colorless, sticky discharge that forms a protective carpet under them as they travel along. The discharge is so effective that they can crawl along the edge of a razor without cutting themselves.

Offered a new pen to write with, 97 percent of all people will write their own name.

Dennis Newton was on trial for the armed robbery of a convenience store in district court when he fired his lawyer. Assistant district attorney Larry Jones said Newton, 47, was doing a fair job of defending himself until the store manager testified that Newton was the robber. Newton jumped up, accused the woman of lying, and then said, "I should have blown your head off." The defendant paused, then quickly added, "If I'd been the one that was there." The jury took 20 minutes to convict Newton and recommended a 30-year sentence.

The "y" in signs reading "ye olde…" is properly pronounced with a "th" sound, not "y." The "th" sound does not exist in Latin, so when ancient Rome occupied (present day) England the rune "thorn" was used to represent "th" sounds.

Spiral staircases in medieval castles run clockwise. This is because all knights used to be right-handed. When the intruding army would climb the stairs they would not be able to use their right hand which was holding the sword because of the difficulties of climbing the stairs. Left-handed knights would have had no troubles, except left-handed people could never become knights because it was assumed that they were descendants of the devil.

Shakespeare spelled his own name several different ways. He is given credit by scholars for introducing as many as 10,000 words and phrases into written language. But it's not at all certain that he made this many words up. Most were probably common terms for his time and he was merely the first to put them in written form in his plays and poems. Some scholars give him credit for thousands, but others say he actually coined only a few hundred. He was the first person to use certain words that are now common, including hurry, alligator, bump, eyeball, and anchovy.

Money man Cornelius Vanderbilt was an insomniac and a believer in the occult. He was not able to fall asleep unless each leg of his bed was planted in a dish filled with salt. He felt this kept out the evil spirits. It also kept out snails, ants, and anyone with high blood pressure.

The giant squid is the largest living creature without a backbone. It weighs up to 2.5 tons and grows up to 55 feet long. Each eye is a foot or more in diameter.

Placing a wreath on a grave is part of an ancient belief that it was necessary to provide comforts for the dead and give them gifts in order for their spirits to not haunt the mourners. The circular arrangement represents a magic circle which is supposed to keep the spirit within its bounds.

Icebergs are not salty—they are comprised of pure fresh water. There may be some dust embedded in the ice, and salt water may cover the surface, but it does not penetrate the ice. Icebergs are quite safe to consume. When an iceberg melts, it makes a fizzing sound. The sound comes from the popping of compressed air bubbles which are in the ice. The bubbles form when air is trapped in the snow layers which are compressed to form glacial ice. The released air is as old as the ice—thousands of years old! Icebergs appear mostly white because of the air bubbles in ice. The bubble surfaces reflect white light, giving the iceberg an overall white appearance. Ice that is bubble-free has a blue tint which is due to the same light phenomenon that tints the sky. In Newfoundland, iceberg ice is "harvested" for bottled water and vodka production.

The world record for a frog jump is 33 feet 5.5 inches over the course of three consecutive leaps, achieved in May, 1977 by a South African sharp-nosed frog called Santjie.

The famous Impressionist painter Claude Monet won 100,000 francs in the state lottery. The money made him financially independent.

Archduke Karl Ludwig (1833–1896), brother of the Austrian emperor, was a man of such piety that on a trip to the Holy Land, he insisted on drinking from the River Jordan, despite warnings that it would make him fatally ill. He died within a few weeks.

Dutch engineers have developed a computerized machine that allows a cow to milk itself. Each cow in the herd has a computer chip in its collar. If the computer senses that the cow has not been milked in a given period of time, the milk-laden animal is allowed to enter the stall. The robot sensors locate the teats, apply the vacuum devices, and the cow is milked. The machine costs a mere $250,000 and is said to boost milk production by 15 percent.

The distinction of being the world's worst driver is a toss-up between two candidates: First, a 75-year-old man who received ten traffic tickets, drove on the wrong side of the road four times, committed four hit-and-run offenses, and caused six accidents, all within 20 minutes on October 15, 1966. Second, a 62-year-old woman who failed her driving test 40 times before passing it in August, 1970. By that time, she had spent over $700 on lessons, and could no longer afford to buy a car.

Influenza got its name from that fact that people believed the disease was caused by the evil "influence" of stars. The worldwide "Spanish flu" epidemic which broke out in 1918 killed more than 30 million people in less than a year.

It's illegal in Alabama to wear a fake mustache that causes laughter in church.

The first country to abolish capital punishment was Austria in 1787.

Charlie Chaplin once won third prize in a Charlie Chaplin look-alike contest.

In the 1700s, European women achieved a pale complexion by eating "Arsenic Complexion Wafers" actually made with the poison.

An itch is a stimulus affecting the nerve endings between the dermis and epidermis; scientists liken it to a form of pain. But that's neither here nor there. It's usually caused by histamine released in the epidermis. Scratching stops it, either by interfering with the nerve impulses or by temporarily damaging the nerves themselves.

The city of St. Petersburg, Russia, was founded in 1703 by Peter the Great, hence the name St. Petersburg. But it wasn't always that simple. In 1914, at the beginning of World War I, Russian leaders felt that Petersburg was too German-sounding. So they changed the name of the city to Petrograd. Then, in 1924, the country's Soviet Communist leaders wanted to honor the founder of the Soviet Union, Vladimir Lenin. The city of Petrograd became Leningrad and was known as Leningrad until 1991, when the new Russian legislators, no longer Soviet Communists, wanted the city to reflect their change of government and changed it back to St. Petersburg.

The *Titanic* was the first ship to use the S.O.S. signal. It was adopted as the international signal for distress in 1912, and the *Titanic* struck the iceberg in April of that year.

Silhouettes are named after a French minister of finance who had a reputation for being tight with money, as silhouettes are a tight outline around a subject.

The first coin-operated machine ever designed was a holy-water dispenser that required a five-drachma piece to operate it. It was the brainchild of the Greek scientist, Hero, in the 1st century A.D.

Fleas can jump more than 200 times their body length and can accelerate 50 times faster than the space shuttle.

The phrase "raining cats and dogs" originated in 17th-century England. During heavy downpours of rain, many of these poor animals unfortunately drowned and their bodies would be seen floating in the rain torrents that raced through the streets. The situation gave the appearance that it had literally rained "cats and dogs" and led to the current expression.

When young and impoverished, Pablo Picasso kept warm by burning his own paintings.

The word encyclopedia is derived from the Greek *enkuklios paideia*, meaning "general education."

You blink every two to ten seconds. As you focus on each word in this sentence, your eyes swing back and forth 100 times a second, and every second the retina performs ten billion computer-like calculations.

Winston Churchill, Prime Minister of England during World War II, superstitiously feared January 24, because he was certain it was destined to be the day of his death. Churchill's father had died on that date. Churchill did indeed die on January 24, 1965.

In parts of Alaska, it's illegal to feed alcohol to a moose, and in Oklahoma, you're subject to fines and/or imprisonment for making "ugly faces" at dogs.

It takes an interaction of 72 different muscles to produce human speech.

In the state of Queensland, Australia, it is still constitutional law that all pubs must have a railing outside for patrons to tie up their horses.

There are at least 805 volcanoes on Earth for which there is at least one eruption with a known date of occurrence. There are 706 more that have had reported eruptions but the dates are unknown. The total number of recorded eruptions on Earth during the past 10,000 years is 7,886. The largest nearby volcano is Olympus Mons on Mars. It is about 17 miles tall. Mount Everest is about six miles tall. The Earth loses most of its heat through volcanoes. Most of the world's volcanoes occur around the east, north, and south sides of the Pacific. The largest volcano in the world is Mauna Loa, Hawaii.

Napoleon's hemorrhoids contributed to his defeat at Waterloo. They prevented him from surveying the battlefield on horseback.

Walt Disney, Tom Cruise, Whoopi Goldberg, Thomas Edison, Henry Winkler, Cher, and Leonardo da Vinci are all famous dyslexics.

A bee could travel four million miles at 7 m.p.h. on the energy it would obtain from one gallon of nectar. Bees have five eyes—there are three small eyes on the top of a bee's head and two larger ones in front. Out of 20,000 species of bees, only four make honey.

In her entire lifetime, Spain's Queen Isabella (1451–1504) bathed twice.

R. C. Gaitlan, 21, walked up to two patrol officers who were showing their squad car computer felon-location equipment to children in a Detroit neighborhood. When he asked how the system worked, the officer asked him for identification. Gaitlan gave them his driver's license; they entered it into the computer and moments later they arrested Gaitlan because information on the screen showed he was wanted for a two-year-old armed robbery in St. Louis, Missouri.

In the U.S., when a drawbridge is open, the only land vehicle that can claim priority over boats is a truck hauling the U.S. mail. This option is seldom if ever exercised, of course.

In ancient Greece, courtesans wore sandals with nails studded into the sole so that their footprints would leave the message "Follow me."

In olden times, to prevent evil spirits from entering the bodies of their male children, parents dressed them in blue. Blue was chosen because it's the color of the sky and was therefore associated with heavenly spirits. Girls weren't dressed in blue, apparently because people didn't think that evil spirits would bother with them. Eventually, however, girls did get their own color: pink. Pink was chosen because of an old English legend which said that girls were born inside of pink roses.

For a while Frederic Chopin, the composer and pianist, wore a beard on only one side of his face. "It does not matter," he explained. "My audience sees only my right side."

Camels have three eyelids to protect themselves from blowing sand.

Although identified with Scotland, bagpipes were actually introduced into the British Isles by the Romans.

Since most people are right-handed, the holes on men's clothes have buttons on the right—to make it easier for men to push them through the holes. Well, that's easy, but aren't women mostly right-handed too? Women's buttons are on the opposite side so their maids can dress them. When buttons were first used, they were expensive and only wealthy women had them. Since a maid faces the woman she is dressing, having the buttons on the left of the dress places them on the maid's right.

The *Mona Lisa* by Leonardo da Vinci is probably the most famous painting in the world. Da Vinci's name for the painting was *La Gioconda*, after the wife of Francesco del Giocondo (1503–06). Who posed for the painting? Dr. Lillian Schwartz of Bell Labs suggests that Leonardo painted himself, and was able to support her theory by analyzing the facial features of Leonardo's face and that of the famous painting. She digitized both the self-portrait of the artist and the *Mona Lisa*. She flipped the self-portrait and merged the two images together using a computer. She noticed the features of the face aligned perfectly.

Tigers have striped skin, not just striped fur.

In 1778, fashionable women of Paris never went out in blustery weather without a lightning rod attached to their hats.

The Alaskan blackfish is found in the Arctic region. When the cold Arctic winter comes, the waters the blackfish calls home freeze. And so does the blackfish! It's not dead, but in a state of suspended animation. Months later when spring arrives, and the ice melts, the blackfish comes back to life and goes swimming off on its merry way as if nothing had happened.

The Chinese developed the custom of using chopsticks because they didn't need anything resembling a knife and fork at the table. They cut up food into bite-sized pieces in the kitchen before serving it. This stemmed from their belief that bringing meat to the table in any form resembling an animal was uncivilized and that it was inhospitable, anyway, to ask a guest to cut food while eating.

The Cairo Opera House was destroyed by fire in 1970. The Cairo fire station was located inside the same building.

Most humans can guess someone's sex with 95 percent accuracy just by smelling their breath.

According to experts, large caves tend to "breathe"; they inhale and exhale great quantities of air when the barometric pressure on the surface changes, and air rushes in or out seeking equilibrium.

More people are killed annually by donkeys than die in air crashes.

The Sarah Winchester house, in San Jose, CA, is a truly bizarre piece of architecture. Mrs. Winchester, after losing first a daughter and then her husband to disease, consulted a medium to find the reason for her terrible luck. The medium advised her that there was a curse on her family, brought about by her late husband's manufacture of rifles. To escape the curse, the medium advised, she should move west and build, and perhaps would live forever. Mrs. Winchester did just that, using the fortune she had inherited to buy a house and just kept building—adding on room after room for 36 years. Each room had 13 windows (the number was considered spiritual rather than unlucky) and many of the windows contained precious jewels. Other odd features of the house, intended to confuse evil spirits, included a staircase that went straight to a ceiling, doors that opened onto two-story drops, a room with a glass floor, and a room without windows that, once entered, a person could not leave without a key. The house contains 160 rooms, 2000 doors, and 10,000 windows, some of which open onto blank walls. There are also secret passageways.

Most common sports drinks are the equivalent of sugar-sweetened human sweat. That is, they have the same salt concentration as sweat (but are less salty than your blood). An increase of as little as one percent in blood salt will cause you to become thirsty.

At age 90, Peter Mustafic of Botovo, Yugoslavia, suddenly began speaking again after a silence of 40 years. The Yugoslavian news agency quoted him as saying, "I just didn't want to do military service, so I stopped speaking in 1920; then I got used to it."

Given their sheer volume, 99 percent of the living space on the planet is found in the oceans. The average depth of the oceans is 2.5 miles. The deepest point lies in the Marianas Trench, 6.8 miles down. By way of comparison, Mount Everest is only 5.5 miles high. If the Earth was smooth, the ocean would cover the entire surface to a depth of 12,000 feet.

Androphobia is fear of men.
Caligynephobia is fear of beautiful women.
Pentheraphobia is fear of a mother-in-law.
Scopophobia is fear of being looked at.
Phobophobia is fear of fearing.
Mageiricophobia is intense fear of having to cook.
Papaphobia is fear of Popes.
Taphephobia is fear of being buried alive.
Clinophobia is fear of beds.

The San Blas Indian women of Panama consider giant noses a mark of great beauty. They paint black lines down the center of their noses to make them appear longer.

High-wire acts have been enjoyed since the time of the ancient Greeks and Romans. Antique medals have been excavated from Greek islands depicting men ascending inclined cords and walking across ropes stretched between cliffs. The Greeks called these high-wire performers neurobates or oribates. In the Roman city of Herculaneum there is a fresco representing a man high on a rope, dancing and playing a flute. Sometimes Roman tightrope walkers stretched cables between the tops of two neighboring hills and performed comic dances and pantomimes while crossing.

While performing her duties as queen, Cleopatra sometimes wore a fake beard.

Charlie Chaplin once reshot a scene in *City Lights* (1931) some 342 times before he felt he had gotten it right. In *Some Like It Hot* (1959), Marilyn Monroe required 59 takes on a scene in which her only line was "Where's the Bourbon?" Similarly, Stanley Kubrick required Shelley Duvall to redo a scene 127 times in *The Shining* (1980).

In the name of art, Chris Burden arranged to be shot by a friend while another person photographed the event. He sold the series of pictures to an art dealer. He made $1750 on the deal, but his hospital bill was $84,000.

While Theodore Roosevelt was campaigning in Milwaukee in 1912, a would-be assassin fired a bullet into the right side of his chest. Much of the force of the bullet was absorbed by the President's eyeglasses case and by the 50-page speech he was carrying double-folded in his breast pocket. Nevertheless, the bullet lodged itself just short of his lung, and, dripping blood, Roosevelt pulled himself up to the podium. He asked the crowd to please "...be very quiet and excuse me from making a long speech. I'll do the best I can, but there's a bullet in my body... I have a message to deliver, and I will deliver it as long as there is life in my body." He spoke for 90 minutes, but was unable to refer to his text due to the gaping hole which the bullet had torn through it.

In a test performed by Canadian scientists, using various different styles of music, it was determined that chickens lay the most eggs when pop music is played.

A couple caught on camera robbing a store could not be identified until the police reviewed the security tape. The woman filled out an entry form for a free trip prior to robbing the store.

Young priests on the island of Leukas, Greece, in order to qualify for service at the temple of Apollo, were required in ancient Greece to don the wings of an eagle and plunge from Cape Dukato into the sea, a dive of 230 feet. It was assumed that the gods would eliminate those unfit, but no diver was ever injured, although the ordeal was performed for centuries.

France has the highest per capita consumption of cheese.

The berry butterflies (*Hypsa monycha*) of Singapore, in their caterpillar stage, group around the top of a stem to foil predatory birds by imitating the appearance of a poisonous berry.

China was the first country to introduce paper money (in A.D. 812), but it wasn't until 1661 that a bank (Banco-Sedlar of Sweden) issued banknotes.

On June 8, 1959, in a move a postal official heralded as "of historic significance to the peoples of the entire world," the Navy submarine *USS Barbero* fired a guided missile carrying 3,000 letters at the Naval Auxiliary Air Station in Mayport, Florida. "Before man reaches the moon," the official was quoted as saying, "mail will be delivered within hours from New York to California, to Britain, to India, or Australia by guided missiles." History proved differently, but this experiment with missile mail exemplifies the pioneering spirit of the Post Office when it came to developing faster, better ways of moving the mail…However, they don't mention if the 3,000 letters were ever delivered.

There are 40,000 muscles and tendons in an elephant's trunk. This makes it very strong and flexible, allowing an elephant to pluck a delicate flower or lift a huge log. The trunk is used for touching, grasping, sucking, spraying, smelling, and striking. Contrary to popular belief, they are not afraid of mice nor is an elephant's memory necessarily the best in the animal kingdom. Although it is not apparent from a distance they are covered with hair. At close range, one can discern a thin coat of light hairs covering practically every part of an elephant's body.

People in Iceland read more books per capita than any other people in the world.

In ancient Japan public contests were held to see who in a town could break wind loudest and longest. Winners were awarded many prizes and received great acclaim.

The custom of saying "Bless you" when someone sneezes was first used by ancients who believed that breath is the essence of life, and when you sneeze a part of your life is escaping. Evil spirits rush into your body and occupy the empty space. By saying "God bless you," the speaker is protecting the sneezer from the evil spirits.

According to *Scientfic American* magazine, if you live in the Northern Hemisphere, odds are that every time you fill your lungs with air at least one molecule of that air once passed through Socrates's lungs.

In Breton, Alabama, there is a law on the town's books against riding down the street in a motorboat.

Mediterranean divers, before the Middle Ages, used to gather the golden strands of the pen shell, using them to weave a very fine cloth for the purpose of making women's gloves. The cloth was so fine, in fact, that a pair of these gloves could be packed into an empty walnut shell, or anything of comparable volume.

In the late 1930s, a man named Abe Pickens of Cleveland, Ohio, attempted to promote world peace by placing personal calls to various country leaders. He managed to contact Mussolini, Hirohito, Franco, and Hitler. Hitler, who didn't understand English, transferred him to an aide. Pickens spent $10,000 to "give peace a chance."

When Gaius Caesar was a boy, Roman soldiers affectionately nicknamed him "little boots" for the boy-sized military footwear he sported. Unfortunately, Gaius grew up and became emperor, incongruously retaining his boyhood diminutive.
"Little boots," in Latin, is "Caligula."

A blue whale's tongue weighs more than an elephant.

The venom of the king cobra is so deadly that one gram of it can kill 150 people. Just handling the substance can put one in a coma.

If the arm of England's King Henry I had been 42 inches long, the unit of measure of a "foot" today would be fourteen inches. But his arm happened to be 36 inches long and he decreed that the "standard" foot should be one-third that length: 12 inches.

The cashew is part of a fruit that grows in tropical regions, called a cashew apple. After harvesting, the cashew apple keeps for only 24 hours before the soft fruit deteriorates. The cashew apple is not commercially important since it spoils quickly, but local people love the fruit. To harvest the nut, the ripe apple is allowed to fall to the ground where natives easily gather it. The apple and nut are separated.

During the Renaissance blonde hair became so *de rigueur* in Venice that a brunette was not to be seen except among the working classes. Venetian women spent hours dyeing and burnishing their hair until they achieved the harsh metallic glitter that was considered a necessity.

The U.S. interstate highway system requires that one mile in every five must be straight. These sections can be used as airstrips in a time of war or other emergencies.

Male monkeys lose the hair on their heads in the same way men do.

A greenish facial tint has long been associated with illness, as suggested by the phrase "green around the gills." As a person who is very envious is considered by many folks to be unwell, these people have been described as "green (or sick) with envy."

The roar that we hear when we place a seashell next to our ear is not the ocean, but rather the sound of blood surging through the veins in the ear. Any cup-shaped object placed over the ear produces the same effect.

The first frozen foods were launched back in the mid-1920s. Clarence Birdseye came up with the idea from his work with the U.S. government surveys of fish and wildlife in Labrador in 1912 and 1915. While working on the surveys, he noted that the natives preserved their fish in ice. He claimed, "I saw natives catching fish in fifty below zero weather, which froze stiff as soon as they were taken out of the water. Months later, when they were thawed out, some of those fish were still alive." Birds Eye's first products were individually boxed packages of peas, cherries, berries, spinach, fish, and meats. Birds Eye products, of course, are still sold. Incan soldiers invented the process of freeze-drying food. The process was primitive but effective— potatoes would be left outside to freeze overnight, then thawed and stomped on to remove excess water.

Toronto's original name was York, but it had another name long before that. The area near the shores of Lake Ontario was called "the meeting place" by the Ojibway of Southern Ontario. Their word: Toronto.

Yucatan, as in the peninsula, is from Mayan "u" + "u" + "uthaan" meaning "listen how they speak," and is what the Mayans said when they first heard the Spaniards.

Police in Radnor, Pennsylvania, interrogated a suspect by placing a metal colander on his head and connecting it with wires to a photocopy machine. The message, "He's lying," was placed in the copier, and police pressed the copy button each time they thought the suspect wasn't telling the truth. Believing the "lie detector" was working, the suspect confessed.

St. Stephen is the patron saint of bricklayers.

In 1931, an industrialist named Robert Ilg built a half-size replica of the Leaning Tower of Pisa outside Chicago and lived in it for several years. The tower is still there.

The ancient Egyptians recommended mixing half an onion with beer foam as a way of warding off death.

"Corduroy" comes from the French, *cord du roi* or "cloth of the king."

After being forced to state in public that the Earth does not rotate, Galileo is said to have muttered under his breath, "Yet it does move."

Male birds actually do most of the singing, primarily to stake out their territory and to invite females of their species over to mate. Females tend to select as mates those male birds who sing the most. It is believed they do this not because they like the quality of the singing, but because they have learned the males who sing the most have the most food in their territory. Since the male doesn't have to spend much time hunting for food, it has more time to sing.

In South America, it would be rude not to ask a man about his wife and children. In most Arab countries, it would be rude to do so. In Sweden, when leaving someone's home, wait until you get to the doorway and step outside before putting on your coat. To do so earlier suggests you are eager to leave. When entering or departing a Russian home, it is considered very bad form to shake hands across the threshold. In Germany, shaking hands with the other hand in a pocket is considered impolite. In Mali, men shake hands with women only if women offer their hand first. The handshake is often done with the left hand touching the other person's elbow as well.

During the reign of Catherine I of Russia, the rules for parties stipulated that no man was to get drunk before 9 o'clock and ladies weren't to get drunk at any hour.

Fourteen years before the *Titanic* sank, novelist Morgan Robertson published a novel called *Futility*. The story was about an ocean liner that struck an iceberg on an April night. The name of the ship in his novel—*The Titan*.

An apple, onion, and potato all have the same taste. The differences in flavor are caused by their smell. To prove this pinch your nose and take a bite from each. They will all taste sweet.

A girl, in the Vacococha tribe of Peru, to prepare her for marriage at the age of 12, is placed in a basket in the hut of her prospective in-laws and must remain suspended over an open fire, night and day for three months.

Hitler was voted *Time* magazine's "Man of the Year" in 1938.

The @ symbol has become an important part of e-mail culture.
It separates the user name from the domain name.
All countries throughout the world use the same symbol
but it obviously has a different name in other tongues.
In English it is simply the "at" sign.
Here are just a few of the more endearing terms:
Italy: "chiocciolina"—which, in Italian, means "little snail."
France: "petit escargot"—also "little snail."
Germany: "klammeraffe"—which means "spider monkey."
Dutch: "api"—a shortened version of "apestaart" or
"monkey's tail."
Finland: "miau" or "cat's tail."
Norway: "kanel-bolle"—a spiral-shaped cinnamon cake.
Israel: "shtrudel"—following the pastry concept.
Denmark: "snabel"—an "A" with a trunk.
Spain: "arroba"—the Spanish symbol for a unit of weight of
about 25 pounds.

An average human drinks about 16,000 gallons of water in a lifetime and uses the bathroom six times per day.

The Vikings believed that the Northern Lights, which are seen from time to time in the north sky, were caused by the flashing armor and spears of Odin's handmaidens as they rode out to collect warriors slain in battle.

The typical person swallows 295 times during dinner.

In Somalia, it's been decreed illegal to carry old chewing gum stuck on the tip of your nose.

"OK" is the most successful of all Americanisms. It has invaded hundreds of other languages and been adopted by them as a word. H. L. Mencken claims that U.S. troops deployed overseas during World War II found it already in use by Bedouins in the Sahara and the Japanese in the Pacific. It was also the fourth word spoken on the surface of the moon. A possiblility is that it stems from "orl korrect," a humorous misspelling of "all correct."

Every time you lick a stamp, you're consuming 1/10 of a calorie. Israeli stamps are certified 100 percent kosher.

In 1961, Henry Matisse's painting *Le Bateau* was hung upside down in New York's Museum of Modern Art. It remained upside down for 41 days until someone noticed. It's estimated nearly 116,000 people passed in front of the painting before the error was noted.

The alarm clock was not invented by the Marquis de Sade, as some suspect, but rather by a man named Levi Hutchins of Concord, New Hampshire, in 1787. Perversity, though, characterized his invention from the beginning. The alarm on his clock could ring only at 4 A.M. Rumor has it that Hutchins was murdered by his wife at 4:05 A.M. on a very dark and cold New England morning.

In the kingdom of Bhutan, all citizens officially become a year older on New Year's Day.

It's a fallacy that owls don't hunt in the daytime because they can't see in daylight. It's just that rats and mice, the main items on owl menus, are most active after dark.

In Northern parts of China it was once a common practice to shave pigs. When the evenings got cold the Chinese would take a pig to bed with them for warmth and found it more comfortable if the pig was clean-shaven.

You can cut up a starfish into pieces and each piece will grow into a completely new starfish.

In medieval times, thunderstorms were believed by some to be the work of demons. So when it stormed, bell-ringers would go up into the bell towers to ring the consecrated bells in an effort to stop the storm. This practice didn't always work out well for the bell-ringer.

Of the world's approximately 5,000 languages, about 2,000 languages are spoken in Papua New Guinea. In Papua New Guinea, there are villages within five miles of each other which speak different languages.

The Chinese ideogram for "trouble" depicts two women living under one roof.

General Henry Heth (1825–1888), leading a Confederate division in the Battle of Gettysburg, was hit in the head by a Union bullet, but his life was saved because he was wearing a hat two sizes too large, with newspaper folded inside the sweatband. The paper deflected the bullet, and the general, unconscious for 30 hours, recovered and lived another 25 years.

Boredom can lead to madness in parrots. When caged by themselves and neglected for long periods of time, these intelligent, sociable birds can easily become mentally ill. Many inflict wounds upon themselves, develop strange tics, and rip out their own feathers. The birds need constant interaction, affection, and mental stimulation; some bird authorities have determined that some parrot breeds have the mental abilities of a five-year-old human child. Should a neglected parrot go mad, there is little that can be done to restore it to normality.

History's first recorded toothpaste was an Egyptian mixture of ground pumice and strong wine. But the early Romans brushed their teeth with human urine, and also used it as a mouthwash. Actually, urine was an active component in toothpaste and mouthwashes until well into the 18th century—the ammonia it contains gave them strong cleansing power.

The first advertisement printed in English in 1477 offered a prayer book. The ad was published by William Caxton on his press in Westminster Abbey. No price was mentioned, only that the book was "good chepe."

The crocodile is surprisingly fast on land. If pursued by a crocodile, a person should run in a zigzag motion, for the crocodile has little or no ability to make sudden changes of direction. The digestive juices of crocodiles contain so much hydrochloric acid that they have dissolved iron spearheads and six-inch steel hooks. A crocodile really does produce tears, but they're not due to sadness. The tears are glandular secretions that work to expel excess salt from the eyes. Hence, "crocodile tears" are false tears.

Americans consume 42 tons of aspirin per day.

An Israeli woman's fight with a stubborn cockroach put her husband in the hospital with burns, a broken pelvis, and broken ribs, *The Jerusalem Post* newspaper reported. The woman, frightened by the insect when she found it in their living room, stepped on it, threw it in a toilet, and sprayed a full can of insecticide on it when it refused to die. Her husband came home from work, went to the toilet, and lit a cigarette. When he threw the cigarette butt into the bowl, the insecticide fumes ignited, "seriously burning his sensitive parts," *The Post* wrote. When paramedics were called to the home in Tel Aviv, they laughed so hard when they learned what had happened that they dropped the stretcher down the stairs, breaking the unidentified man's pelvis and ribs.

A bird "chews" with its stomach. Since most birds do not have teeth, a bird routinely swallows small pebbles and gravel. These grits become vigorously agitated in the bird's stomach and serve to grind food as it passes through the digestive system.

The Main Library at Indiana University sinks over an inch every year because, when it was built, engineers failed to take into account the weight of all the books that would occupy the building.

Women blink nearly twice as much as men.

It's physically impossible for you to lick your elbow.

In New York City there are more people of Irish descent than in Dublin, Ireland, more people of Italian descent than in Rome, Italy, and more Jews than in Tel Aviv, Israel.

Canadian actor Charles Coghlan died in 1899 in Galveston, Texas, around 3,480 miles from his home on Prince Edward Island. He was buried in a lead coffin which was placed in a granite vault. In 1900, a hurricane hit Galveston. The vault where Coghlan was buried was flooded and his coffin floated out into the Bay of Mexico and then out into the Atlantic Ocean. The Gulf Stream carried it along for eight years until October 1908 when it was spotted by a local fisherman on Prince Edward Island. Coghlan's body had returned home nine years after his death.

A crocodile cannot stick its tongue out.

In 1555, Ivan the Terrible ordered the construction of St. Basil's Cathedral in Moscow. He was so thrilled with the work done by the two architects that he had them blinded so they could never be able to build anything else more beautiful.

The expression "getting someone's goat" is based on the custom of keeping a goat in the stable with a racehorse as the horse's companion. The goat becomes a settling influence on the thoroughbred. If you owned a competing horse and were not above some dirty business, you could steal your rival's goat (seriously, it's been done) to upset the other horse and make it run a poor race. From goats and horses it was linguistically extended to people: in order to upset someone, "get their goat."

Despite a population of over a billion, China has only about 200 family names.

The world's largest art gallery is the Winter Palace and Hermitage in St. Petersburg, Russia. Visitors would have to walk 15 miles to see the 322 galleries which house nearly three million works of art.

The electric chair was invented by a dentist.

TYPEWRITER is the longest word that can be made using the letters on only one row of the keyboard.

The ancient Romans built such an excellent system of roads that the saying arose "all roads lead to Rome," that is, no matter which road one starts a journey on, he will finally reach Rome if he keeps on traveling. The popular saying came to mean that all ways or methods of doing something end in the same result, no method being better than another.

Traffic engineering was developed in ancient Rome as well. The Appian Way, for example, stretched 350 miles from the Eternal City to Brundisium. In Rome itself there were actually stop signs and even alternate-side-of-the-street parking.

The first VCR, made in 1956, was the size of a piano.

The smallest book in the Library of Congress is *Old King Cole*. It is 1/25-of-an-inch by 1/25-of-an-inch. The pages can only be turned with the use of a needle.

White elephants were rare even in Siam (modern Thailand). If you found one the emperor automatically owned it and you couldn't harm it. When the emperor wanted to punish someone, he gave him or her a white elephant as a gift. The person couldn't ride it or work it, but still had to take care of it and clean up after it. So the gift was useless. Hence the expression.

Antarctica is the only continent that does not have land areas below sea level.

Flamingo tongues were a common delicacy at Roman feasts.

In Kentucky, two men tried to pull the front off a cash machine by running a chain from the machine to the bumper of their pickup truck. Instead of pulling the front panel off the machine, though, they pulled the bumper off their truck. Scared, they left the scene and drove home, leaving the chain still attached to the machine. With their bumper still attached to the chain. With their vehicle's license plate still attached to the bumper.

A snail can sleep for three years.

Gordon Bennett, whose name became an expletive, was born in 1841. By the age of 25 he was earning over a million dollars a year after taxes. He got through over 40 million dollars in his lifetime. He paid $2,000,000 for a yacht which had a specially designed room for an Alderney cow to supply him with fresh milk. He once tipped a porter $14,000 and bought a Monte Carlo restaurant on the spot when he arrived to find his regular table was occupied. He had the offending party evicted, sat down at his table, and gave the restaurant to one of the waiters. He was the man who commissioned Stanley to find Livingstone.

The flesh of the puffer fish (*fugu*) is considered a delicacy in Japan. It is prepared by chefs specially trained and certified by the government to prepare the flesh free of the toxic liver, gonads, and skin. Despite these precautions, many cases of tetrodotoxin poisoning are reported each year in patients ingesting fugu. Poisonings usually occur after eating fish caught and prepared by uncertified handlers. The end result, in most cases, is death.

In 10 minutes, a hurricane releases more energy than all of the world's nuclear weapons combined.

It's possible to lead a cow upstairs…but not downstairs.

The cigarette lighter was invented before the match.

Without using precision instruments, Eratosthenes measured the radius of Earth in the 3rd century B.C., and came within one percent of the value determined by today's technology.

Elephants are the only animals that can't jump.

In Los Angeles, discarded garments are being recycled as industrial rags and carpet underlay. Such recycling keeps clothing out of landfills, where it makes up 4 percent of the trash dumped each year.

Our eyes are always the same size from birth, but our noses and ears never stop growing.

If Barbie were life-size, her measurements would be 39-23-33. She would stand seven-feet, two-inches tall.

Butterflies taste with their feet.

To clean tarnished copper bottoms of pots and pans, spread a little ketchup onto the bottom. Let it sit for about one minute. Wipe it clean and rinse.

The Associated Press reported in December 1985, in Eugene, Oregon, a six-month old kitten set a Christmas tree on fire while batting at the lighted bulbs. The heat of the fire cracked a nearby fishbowl, and water from the bowl doused some of the fire. Firefighters arrived within minutes of the fire starting and put out the fire, which had spread to the carpet. A goldfish named Clyde was found lying prone in the cracked bowl, and when put into another bowl with water, was quickly revived and survived the ordeal. The water in Clyde's bowl had prevented the fire from getting out of control.

Ancient Chinese artists would never paint pictures of women's feet.

Here are some of the many Eskimo words for snow:

apun	snow
apingaut	first snowfall
aput	spread-out snow
kanik	frost
kanigruak	frost on a living surface
ayak	snow on clothes
kannik	snowflake
nutagak	powder snow
aniu	packed snow
aniuvak	snowbank
natigvik	snowdrift
kimaugruk	snowdrift that blocks something
perksertok	drifting snow
akelrorak	newly drifting snow
mavsa	snowdrift overhead and about to fall
kaiyuglak	rippled surface of snow
pukak	sugar snow
pokaktok	salt-like snow
miulik	sleet
massak	snow mixed with water
auksalak	melting snow
aniuk	snow for melting into water
akillukkak	soft snow
milik	very soft snow
mitailak	soft snow covering an ice floe opening
sillik	hard crusty snow
kiksrukak	glazed snow in a thaw
mauya	snow that can be broken through
katiksunik	light snow
katiksugnik	light snow deep enough for walking
apuuak	snow patch
sisuuk	avalanche!

On average, 100 people choke to death on ball-point pens every year.

Thirty-five percent of the people who use personal ads for dating are already married.

A full moon rarely shows up on Halloween, although Halloween is often associated with full moons. Full moons on Halloween over the past century have occurred in 1925, 1944, 1955, and 1974. The next full moon on October 31 will occur in 2020.

The size of the first footprint on the moon was thirteen-by-six inches, the dimensions of Neil Armstrong's boot, when he took his historic walk on July 20, 1969.

There is an organization in Berkeley, California, whose members gather monthly to discuss and honor the garlic plant. Called The Lovers of the Stinky Rose, this unusual organization holds an annual garlic festival and publishes a newsletter known as *Garlic Time*.

The air is so polluted in Cubato, Brazil, that no birds or insects remain, most trees are blackened stumps, and its mayor reportedly refuses to live there.

A space shuttle at lift-off develops more power than all the automobiles in England combined.

About 99 percent of pumpkins marketed domestically are used as jack-o'-lanterns at Halloween.

An organization called SCROOGE was formed in 1979 in Charlottesville, Virginia. The acronym stands for the Society to Curtail Ridiculous, Outrageous, and Ostentatious Gift Exchanges.

In Calama, a town in the Atacama Desert of Chile, it has never rained.

A beautiful mirage called the Fata Morgana appears in the Straits of Messina, between Sicily and Italy. It is an image of a town in the sky, but it seems more like a fairy landscape than a real town. It is believed to be a mirage of a fishing village situated along the coast.

The Adventures of Tom Sawyer, by Mark Twain, was the first novel ever to be written on a typewriter.

When out hiking or camping, you can determine how much daylight is left by holding your fist up to the western horizon. Stack your fists on top of one another up to the Sun's level in the sky. Each fist represents about an hour of remaining daylight.

A duck's quack doesn't echo, and no one knows why.

The banana cannot reproduce itself. It can be propagated only by the hand of man.

There are more than 700 species of garden plants that have been identified as dangerous if eaten. Among them are the buttercup, daffodil, lily of the valley, sweet pea, oleander, azalea, bleeding heart, delphinium, and rhododendron.

There is about one quarter-pound of salt in every gallon of seawater.

Fingerprints serve a function—they provide traction for the fingers to grasp things. Koalas and humans are the only animals with unique prints. Koala prints cannot be distinguished from human fingerprints.

In 1972, a group of scientists reported that you could cure the common cold by freezing the big toe.

The planet Venus does not tilt as it goes around the sun, so consequently, it has no seasons. On Mars, however, the seasons are more exaggerated and last much longer than on Earth.

There is one mile of railroad track in Belgium for every one-and-a-half square miles of land.

The Boston Nation, a newspaper published in Ohio during the mid-19th century, had pages seven-and-a-half feet long and five-and-a-half feet wide. It required two people to hold the paper in proper reading position.

There is one slot machine in Las Vegas for every eight inhabitants.

Studies of the Dead Sea Scrolls indicate that the passage in the Bible known as the Sermon on the Mount is actually an ancient Essene prayer dating to hundreds of years before the birth of Christ.

The bark of the redwood tree is fireproof. Fires in redwood forests take place inside the trees.

In living memory, it was not until February 18, 1979, that snow fell on the Sahara. The half-hour storm in southern Algeria stopped traffic. But within a few hours, all the snow had melted.

The biggest snowflake ever reported measured 15 inches across.

A "hairsbreadth away" is 1/48 of an inch.

In the Middle Ages, the highest court in France ordered the execution of a cow for injuring a human.

The United States has the rest of the world beat when it comes to its toilets. Per a survey of 100 international travel writers, the United States has, by far, the best in the world. Western Europe may have the best castles and museums, but johns finished a distant second. Scandinavia, rated separately from Western Europe, placed third. China's bathrooms are considered the absolute worst according to the surveyed travel writers. Almost as bad are those toilets in the Middle East and the former Soviet Union. The Soviet Union was also voted the worst when it comes to toilet paper.

There are 170,000,000,000,000,000,000,000,000 ways to play the ten opening moves in a game of chess.

A bucket filled with earth would weigh about five times more than the same bucket filled with the substance of the sun. However, the force of gravity is so much greater on the sun that a man weighing 150 pounds on our planet would weigh two tons on the sun.

There were 15,700,003 Model T Fords manufactured, all in black.

A cosmic year is the amount of time it takes the sun to revolve around the center of the Milky Way, about 225 million years.

The African baobab tree can have a circumference as large as 100 feet. One such tree in Zimbabwe is so wide that the hollowed-out trunk serves as a shelter at a bus stop, with a capacity to hold as many as 40 people.

Celery has negative calories—it takes more calories to eat and digest a piece of celery than the celery has in it initially.

Of about 350 million cans of chicken noodle soup of all commercial brands sold annually in the United States, 60 percent is purchased during the cold and flu season. January is the top-selling month of the year.

In ancient Egypt, onions were an object of worship. The onion symbolized eternity to the Egyptians, who buried onions along with their Pharaohs. The anatomy of the onion suggested a circle-within-a-circle structure, symbolizing eternal life.

American sculptor Alexander Calder rigged the front door of his Paris apartment so that he could open it from his bathtub.

Paper can be made from asparagus.

Parsley is a common herb of the Mediterranean area and was well known to the ancient Greeks. They considered it too sacred to eat. Romans did serve it as a garnish and to improve the taste of food. They believed it had special powers and would keep them sober.

Alfred Nobel of Stockholm, Sweden, patented dynamite in 1867.

The shortest human we have documented evidence on was Pauline Musters of the Netherlands. She measured 12 inches at her birth in 1876, and was 23 inches tall with a weight of nine pounds at her death in 1895.

The father of the pink flamingo (the plastic lawn ornament) was Don Featherstone of Massachusetts. Featherstone graduated from art school and went to work as a designer for Union Products, a Leominster, Massachusetts, company that manufactured flat plastic lawn ornaments. He designed the pink flamingo in 1957 as a follow-up project to his plastic duck. The company sells an average of 250,000 to 500,000 plastic pink flamingos a year.

U.S. Patent #D219,584 was issued in 1970 to veteran movie actor Steve McQueen. He was famous not only for his movies but also for racing cars and working on engines off-camera as well. A byproduct of his racing hobby was the invention of a bucket seat.

Cockney rhyming slang began in London around the 1850s as a statement of independence felt by those who prided themselves on having been born within the sound of Bow Bells, the bells of London's Bow Church.

An Englishman invented Scotland's national dress—the kilt. It was developed from the philamore, a massive piece of tartan worn with a belt and draped over the shoulder, by English industrialist Thomas Rawlinson. Rawlinson ran a foundry at Lochaber, Scotland, in the early 1700s, and thought a detachable garment would make life more comfortable for his workers.

Although it took less than a decade of space travel for man to get to the moon, 19th- and 20th-century engineers needed 22 years to design the zipper.

It is the female lion who does more than 90 percent of the hunting, while the male is afraid to risk his life, or simply prefers to rest.

A space vehicle must move at a rate of at least 17 miles per second to escape Earth's gravitational pull. This is equivalent to going from New York to Philadelphia in about 20 seconds.

The Leap-The-Dips roller coaster is the oldest roller coaster in the world. It is located within Lakemont Park in Pennsylvania. It was built in 1902, the largest dip is 9 feet, and the steepest dip descent is 25 degrees. The average ride time of Leap-The-Dips is one minute and the average speed is ten miles per hour.

There are no clocks in Las Vegas gambling casinos.

The piece that protrudes from the top end of an umbrella is called a "ferrule." The word "ferrule" is also used to describe the piece of metal that holds a rubber eraser on a pencil.

The name "piano" is an abbreviation of Cristofori's original name for the instrument: "piano et forte," or "soft and loud."

Two chapters in the Bible, 2 Kings and Isaiah 37, are alike almost word for word.

The name of the legendary Lady Godiva's horse was Aethenoth.

The name of the ornament atop the hood of every Rolls Royce car is the Spirit of Ecstasy.

U.S. congressmen expressed surprise on learning in 1977 that it takes 15 months of instruction at the Pentagon's School of Music to turn out a bandleader, but merely 13 months to train a jet pilot.

All the proceeds earned from James M. Barrie's book *Peter Pan* were bequeathed to the Great Ormond Street Hospital for Sick Children in London.

The human brain is about 85 percent water.

The blood of mammals is red, the blood of insects is yellow, and the blood of lobsters is blue.

The names of Popeye's four nephews are Pipeye, Peepeye, Pupeye, and Poopeye.

Both Shakespeare and Cervantes died on the same day— April 23, 1616.

Brontology is the study of thunder.

The Procrastinators' Club of America sends news to its members under the masthead *Last Month's Newsletter*.

Great Britain was the first country in the world to issue postage stamps, and it's the only nation in the world today that doesn't use a national name on its stamps.

A dog was killed by a meteor at Nakhla, Egypt, in 1911. The unlucky canine is the only creature known to have been killed by a meteor.

Green Bay, Wisconsin lays claim to being "The Toilet Paper Capital of The World."

In 18th-century English gambling dens, there was an employee whose only job was to swallow the dice if there was a raid.

The average person walks the equivalent of twice around the world in a lifetime.